BookLife PUBLISHING

©2019
BookLife Publishing Ltd.
King's Lynn
Norfolk, PE30 4LS

All rights reserved.
Printed in Malaysia.

A catalogue record for this book is available from the British Library.

ISBN: 978-1-78637-858-3

Written by:
Shalini Vallepur

Edited by:
Madeline Tyler

Designed by:
Gareth Liddington

All facts, statistics, web addresses and URLs in this book were verified as valid and accurate at time of writing.

No responsibility for any changes to external websites or references can be accepted by either the author or publisher.

With thanks to Robin Twiddy, William Anthony and Emilie Dufresne.

Are you ready to learn about the things we got up to in ancient Egypt? Read on and I'll tell you about some of the things we did.

PHOTO CREDITS

All images are courtesy of Shutterstock.com, unless otherwise specified. With thanks to Getty Images, Thinkstock Photo and iStockphoto. Front Cover – zizi_mentos, Meilun, Macrovector, Alfmaler, VectorShow, matrioshka, Tomacco, Nadya_Art. 4&5 – Ewa Studio, Filippo Vanzo, Plateresca, 6&7 - NotionPic, Stoyan G. Ivanov, Knhlhilee9898, AndreyO. 8&9 - Evil Khan, maradon 333, ru.wikipedia, Zbigniew Guzowski, Alensha, Budge, E. A. Wallis, OTRS, Shanvood, 10&11 - Vectors Bang, Whyimage, askmove konstantin, British Museum, 12&13 - Egyptian Studio, Rama, Tim UR, lady-luck, Jim Hedd, 14&15 - Jeff Dahl, WitR, The Oxford Encyclopedia, Boston Museum, tan_tan, Merydolla, 16&17 - Frederick P. Huntley Bequest, agsaz, Wellcome Images, Anatolir, GoodStudio, SlyBrowney, Natsmith1, Metropolitan Museum of Art, Olga Kuevda, Keith Schengili-Roberts, 18&19 - NotionPic, Kaldari, notkoo, Chongsiri Chaitongngam, 20&21 - Daderot, Nina de Garis Davies, ddenisen, Zde, Pudpon, 22&23 - Lars Poyansky, Jose Ignacio Soto, Bildangentur Zoonar mbH, Hugh R. Hopgood, Andrii_M, 24&25 - Guillaume Blanchard, fae, Pharos, AnnstasAg, AVIcon, Leoboudv, 26&27 - Esterel13, Max Pixel, Pharos, AndreasPraefcke, 28&29 - Kaldari, Karen Green, Niall O'Donoghue, Edgardo Ariel Rodriguez, matrioshka.

CONTENTS

Page 4	Welcome to Ancient Egypt!
Page 6	The Gods
Page 8	Worship
Page 10	Mummies
Page 12	Medicine and More
Page 14	Fierce Pharaohs
Page 16	Cool and Clean
Page 17	Hair Is for the Foolish
Page 18	Precious Pets
Page 20	Fun and Games
Page 22	The World of Hieroglyphs
Page 24	House and Home
Page 26	Children Did What?
Page 28	Crime and Punishment
Page 30	Senebti!
Page 31	Glossary
Page 32	Index

Words that look like THIS are explained in the glossary on page 31.

Welcome to Ancient Egypt!

Em hotep! That's how we said 'hello' in ancient Egyptian. When we talk about ancient Egypt, we mean the time between 3150 BC and 30 BC – that's over 3,000 years of ancient Egyptian antics.

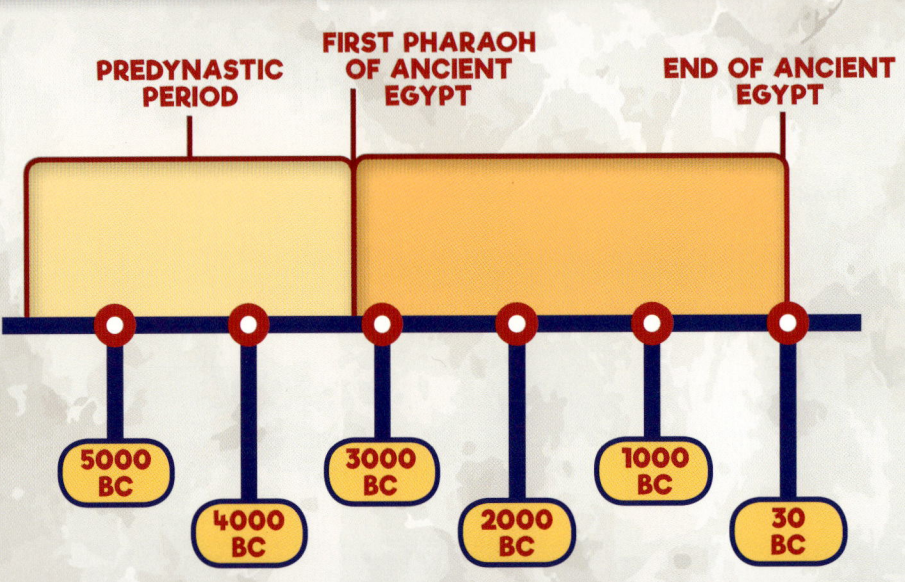

PREDYNASTIC PERIOD | FIRST PHARAOH OF ANCIENT EGYPT | END OF ANCIENT EGYPT

5000 BC • 4000 BC • 3000 BC • 2000 BC • 1000 BC • 30 BC

Ancient Egyptian CIVILISATION started growing around 5000 BC. The time before 3100 BC is called the predynastic period, and it's before we had any kings or pharaohs.

THE NILE

Ancient Egyptians chose to live near the River Nile. Thanks to the Nile, ancient Egyptian civilisation was able to grow and last for such a long time. We didn't get a lot of rain in ancient Egypt. The Nile gave us water and FERTILE soil to grow food on. We also used it to travel.

River Nile

ANCIENT CITIES

Most ancient Egyptians lived in cities. Many different cities took their turn at being the capital city of ancient Egypt. The capital city was the main city in ancient Egypt at the time.

WHO'S WHO IN ANCIENT EGYPT?

There were lots of different people in ancient Egypt, but not everybody was treated the same.

Pharaoh – People believed the pharaoh was like a god. The pharaoh led ancient Egypt and made all the big decisions.

Viziers – Viziers worked under the pharaoh and collected <u>TAXES</u>.

Priests and nobles – Priests were important because they helped to keep the gods happy, and nobles made sure things ran smoothly where they lived.

Scribes – Scribes could read and write, and they kept <u>RECORDS</u> of important things.

Soldiers and craftspeople – Soldiers fought in wars and craftspeople made all sorts of things.

Farmers and peasants – Farmers grew food and looked after animals.

Slaves – We had slaves that usually worked in our houses or in <u>MINES</u>.

The Gods

The gods and goddesses were huge parts of our lives. We had gods that looked after certain parts of life. We needed to worship all the gods to make sure we had happy lives.

Ra:	God of the Sun, shown as a man with the head of a hawk who travelled across the sky during the day
Osiris:	God of the underworld and death, had green skin and was murdered by Seth
Anubis:	God of the dead, shown as a man with the head of a **JACKAL** and was linked with mummies
Isis:	Goddess of protection, healing and children and was the wife of Osiris
Amun:	Chief of the gods, created the universe and was often shown having a ram's head
Mut:	Goddess of the sky and was often shown as a woman wearing a crown
Horus:	God of the sky, son of Osiris and Isis and was sometimes shown as a man with the head of a falcon
Thoth:	God of the Moon, learning and writing and was often shown to have the head of a bird
Hathor:	Goddess of women, love and beauty and was often shown having a cow's head
Sekhmet:	Goddess of war, destruction and healing and was often shown having the head of a lioness
Geb:	God of Earth, father of Osiris, Isis and Seth, his laughter was believed to cause earthquakes
Seth:	God of darkness and **CHAOS**, Seth murdered his brother Osiris

We believed in over 2,000 gods and goddesses.

SETH DID WHAT?!

It was hard to keep track of what the gods were up to because they were always fighting with each other. Seth was jealous that Osiris was king, so he tore Osiris into 42 little pieces. Isis, Osiris's wife, tried her best to put Osiris back together, but she could only find 41 pieces of Osiris. How horrible!

RA DID WHAT?

Ancient Egyptians believed that for the Sun to rise, Ra had to fight the demon Apep every day. On the days that Ra won the fight, the Sun would shine, and on the days Apep won the fight, there would be grey skies and storms. If there was an eclipse, it meant that Apep had swallowed Ra.

Apep

Worship

PRIESTS

Pharaohs built TEMPLES to different gods, and these temples were looked after by priests. Priests performed all sorts of RITUALS to keep the gods happy and protect ancient Egypt.

THE CROC MUMMY

We gave many gifts to the gods. The god Sobek was shown as a crocodile. Crocodiles were turned into mummies and placed in temples to Sobek to please him. Some crocodile mummies were stuffed full of baby crocodile mummies.

Read more about mummies on page 10!

8

SACRIFICES

It was believed that some ancient Egyptians offered more than just animals to the gods – people were offered too. During the predynastic times, people were <u>SACRIFICED</u> to the gods. They were usually criminals who were being punished.

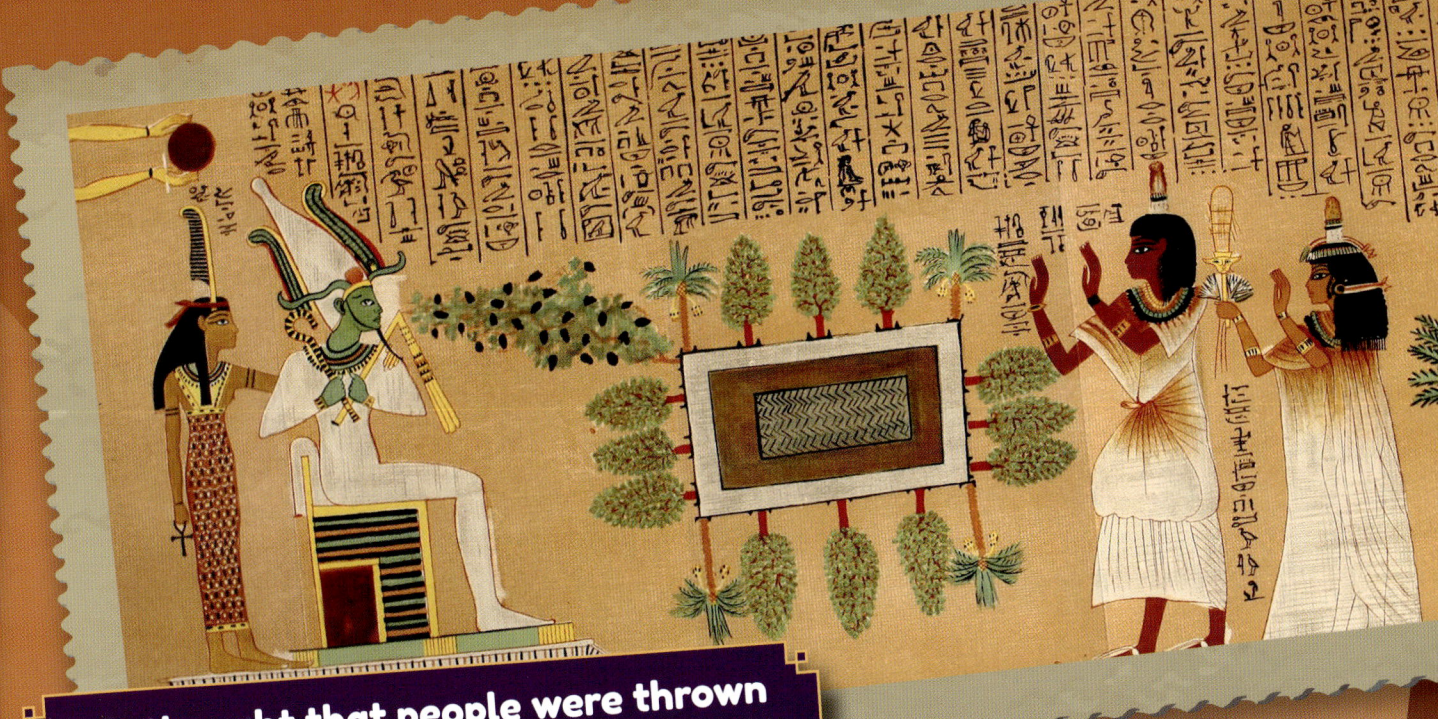

It is thought that people were thrown into the River Nile as a sacrifice.

THE SACRED SCARAB

Scarabs, also known as dung beetles, were worshipped in ancient Egypt. They rolled balls of poo around to eat. The balls of poo reminded us of the Sun.

Lots of pieces of jewellery had scarabs on them.

Mummies

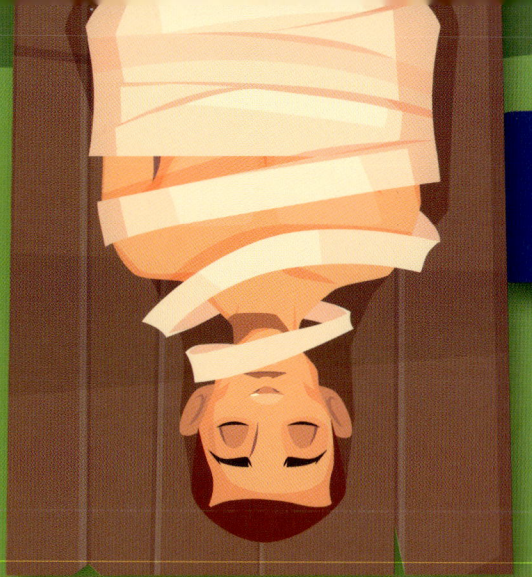

Ancient Egyptians believed that people went to the **AFTERLIFE** when they died. Bodies had to be **PRESERVED**, or mummified, in order for them to make it there safely.

MAKING A MUMMY

Rich ancient Egyptians could afford to be preserved in a different way to poorer people. Let's take a look at the different ways that mummies were made.

FOR THE RICH:

1. Make a cut on the side of the belly and remove the **ORGANS**.
2. Use a hooked tool to remove the brain through the nose – be careful not to damage the face!
3. Put lots of **MYRRH** and spices inside the belly and sew the cut up.
4. Cover the body in **NATRON** and leave it for 70 days.
5. Wash the body and roll it in **LINEN**.

FOR THE POOR:

1. Make a cut on the side of the belly and remove the organs.
2. Cover the body in natron and leave it for 70 days.
3. Give the body back to the family.

Organs were preserved in canopic jars that were shaped like the gods.

COFFINS, CARVINGS AND SARCOPHAGI

Most mummies were placed in coffins. Coffins were usually rectangular boxes, but some people were buried in fancy coffins shaped like a person. The coffin was placed in a sarcophagus which was usually a big, stone container. Rich people had sarcophagi that had eyes or other pictures painted on them. We believed that the mummy inside could use these eyes to see outside the sarcophagus.

Fancy coffin

Turn to page 14 to see how pharaohs were buried.

THE BOOK OF THE DEAD

The Book of the Dead helped us find our way to the Field of Reeds in the afterlife. Getting to the Field of Reeds was no easy task. We had to get past a giant SERPENT, meet and talk to different gods and face different tests. People could ask a priest for their own book to be made before they died. The book was full of spells, tips and tricks for getting to the afterlife safely.

In one test, Anubis would weigh the dead person's heart and an ostrich feather. If the heart weighed more than the feather, well, let's just say the person wouldn't have a good time in the afterlife.

That is one heavy feather.

Medicine and More

CHANNELS

Ancient Egyptians believed that a person got ill when the gods were angry with them. We believed that the gods blocked CHANNELS in the body which stopped things flowing properly. This would cause all sorts of problems.

We thought that channels in the body were a bit like channels in crop fields.

DIARRHOEA ALERT!

If somebody was ill, it meant that a channel somewhere in their body was blocked. Giving somebody LAXATIVES was the best way to unblock a channel. It meant that the person had horrible DIARRHOEA, but at least their channels were unblocked!

Figs were used to make people poo.

What beautiful teeth she had!

12

MAGIC CURES

Stopping illnesses before they happened was just as important as curing them. AMULETS were magical and we believed that they stopped us from getting ill. They came in all sorts of different shapes. Bedwetting was easily cured by wearing mouse bones around the neck.

Amulets

TO THE DENTIST

There were many doctors in ancient Egypt and there were even a few dentists. We needed dentists because the bread we ate was so rough, it wore our teeth down! If a tooth fell out of somebody's mouth, an ancient Egyptian dentist used a bit of wire to put it back in.

Fierce Pharaohs

The pharaoh was the most powerful person in ancient Egypt. He or she was the ruler of ancient Egypt and had control over what happened. We believed that the pharaoh was the god Horus living among us.

Fake beard

SCEPTRE

PYRAMID POWER

As soon as a pharaoh came into power, they started to get ready for their death. No, seriously – pharaohs were buried in huge pyramids and it took years to build them, so they had to start planning early.

Some pharaohs wore fake beards to look more like a god and carried a sceptre to look more powerful.

Pharaoh tombs were decorated with paintings like this.

14

PEPI DID WHAT?

Pharaoh Pepi II became a pharaoh when he was six years old. According to legend, there was nothing he hated more than flies. He hated flies so much that he covered two naked slaves in honey and had them stand near him at all times. This way, all the annoying flies would get stuck to the slaves and Pepi would be free of flies.

"The flies won't leave me alone, Mum!"

"RUN!"

"Quick, run! He's getting the honey out again!"

"Mess with me and I'll walk all over you."

TUT DID WHAT?

Pharaoh Tutankhamun wore very special sandals. His sandals had his enemies painted on them. With every step he took, Tut squashed his enemies to the ground.

Cool and Clean

Looking good was important. Ancient Egyptians bathed every day in the River Nile or in baths at home. Men and women wore a type of eyeliner called kohl to protect their eyes from sunlight and to look good.

Pharaohs had special baths like these where the water could be kept warm.

Pot of kohl

BEAUTIFUL SMILES

We had our own toothpaste. The recipe was simple, although a bit scratchy, and it kept our teeth squeaky clean.

Terrific Toothpaste Ingredients:

- **Powdered ox HOOVES**
- **Ashes**
- **Burnt eggshells**
- **Pumice stone**

16

Hair Is for the Foolish

Being bald was better than being hairy in ancient Egypt. People that kept their hair had to deal with **LICE**. Men, women and children removed the hair from their heads to avoid lice. We used **RAZORS** or pumice stones to rub the hair away.

I feel pretty, oh so pretty!

WONDERFUL WIGS

Even though we shaved our heads, many people still wanted hair on their heads, so they wore wigs. Wigs were very popular among women. They wore wigs that were made of sheep's wool. Rich people had wigs that were made of human hair.

Some wigs had gold woven into them.

Some people were buried with copper razors so they could keep things trimmed in the afterlife.

Precious Pets

The ancient Egyptians had lots of weird and wonderful pets. They kept anything, from dogs and cats to lions and gazelles. Some animals were so important to the Egyptians that they worshipped them.

I am Tiddles. Worship me!

FACT Bastet was the goddess of cats.

I want to be on my own, please. Can't you see my eyebrows have gone?

GOOD MOURNING!

Cats were the most precious pets of all to the ancient Egyptians. They were worshipped as protectors of the home they lived in. Cats were so special that when they died, their owners shaved off their own eyebrows to MOURN their loss.

MONKEY BUTLERS

Have you ever needed something but didn't want to move to get it? This might not have been a problem if you were an ancient Egyptian. Some ancient Egyptians kept pet monkeys. The monkeys were trained to find and fetch things for their owners.

I get paid in hugs. I'd prefer cash, if I'm honest.

EXTREME PETS

The ancient Egyptians were not afraid of keeping some very dangerous animals as pets. If you were a rich Egyptian, you might have bought yourself a terrifying lion or a snapping crocodile.

Keep still, human. Biting in 3... 2... 1...

Fun and Games

MEHEN

Mehen was the best. The board looked like a coiled-up snake. Six people could play it at the same time. Each person had to pick a playing piece that was in the shape of an animal. I always chose to be the hippopotamus, but there were also dog and lion pieces.

FACT
Mehen was a serpent god who protected Ra.

Snaky mehen board

Queen Nefertiti was painted on the walls of her tomb playing senet.

SENET

Senet was one of the oldest games we had. It was a bit like a racing game where players had to beat challenges. The game represented the tasks that people had to do to get into the afterlife. Because of this, some people had senet games painted on the walls of their tomb.

20

HOCKEY

Sports were an important part of our lives. They kept us fit and healthy. We played a game that was a bit like hockey. We made the bats out of palm tree branches and whacked a ball that was made from papyrus.

TUG-OF-HOOPS

We had our own type of tug-of-war. We didn't play it with a rope, but used hoops. Each player carried a long stick that had a hook on the end. The hoop was placed on the ground and a line was drawn underneath it. Players used their sticks to pull the hoop. The first person to pull the hoop over their side of the line won the game.

The World of Hieroglyphs

We had our own writing system called hieroglyphs. Hieroglyphs were pictures that usually represented a sound, but some represented full words, objects or feelings. Take a look at some of the hieroglyphs we used.

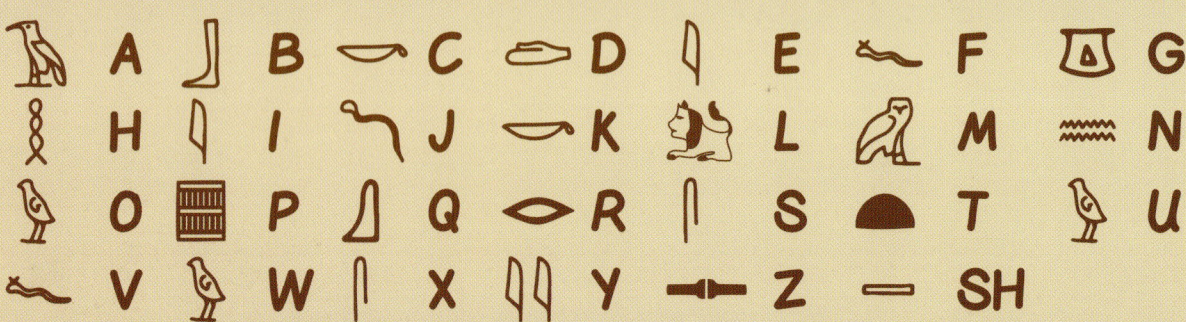

There were over 1,000 hieroglyphs! These are just a few.

I get to sit and write all day!

THE LIFE OF A SCRIBE

Not many people in ancient Egypt could read and write. Scribes used hieroglyphs and wrote down all the important things for everybody else. People were selected to become scribes when they were children. They were sent to a special school to learn all the different hieroglyphs.

PAPYRUS PAPER

Hieroglyphs were carved onto certain objects, such as sarcophagi and walls. We also had our own type of paper to write on. It was made from a plant called papyrus. It grew near the Nile and was HARVESTED by workers who would cover the plant with linen and squash it until it became like paper.

Papyrus

SECRET MESSAGE

I had hieroglyphs written on the walls of my tomb, but I can't read what they say! Could you use the table and find out what they say?

Does it say something nice?

Hieroglyph message: I HOPE YOU HAVE LICE FOREVER

23

House and Home

Most ancient Egyptians lived in houses that were made from mud bricks. Making bricks was easy. Workers took mud, shaped it into bricks and left them out in sunlight to dry. Some rich people lived in stone houses. The really rich people had their own swimming pools.

Some houses looked like this.

HEAD AND SHOULDERS

After a hard day at work, ancient Egyptians looked forward to going home and going to bed. Our pillows were the comfiest. They were made of stone! If you didn't have a pillow, then you would enjoy resting your head against the floor because this is where most ancient Egyptians slept.

Really rich people had pillows like these. Comfy right?

A GIRAFFE SOLUTION

Flies were a big problem in ancient Egypt. They loved coming into our houses and causing trouble. We covered our windows and door with papyrus mats, but this wasn't enough. We took the tail off a giraffe and used it to chase flies away. Bring in the giraffe flyswatter!

TOILET TROUBLES

Most ancient Egyptians didn't have nice toilets. A hole in the ground with a stool on top was the best way to go. While most people used these toilets, it's believed that rich Egyptians had big bathrooms and toilets made of LIMESTONE in their homes.

Limestone toilet seat

Children Did What?

What did children get up to in ancient Egypt? Children were thought of as gifts from the gods. If people couldn't have children of their own, they could ADOPT some. Most children got to play around until they were five years old.

Most children walked around totally naked.

OFF TO SCHOOL

Only a few boys got to go to school. They started school when they were around five years old and usually finished when they were 14. They were taught all kinds of subjects such as history and maths. When they left school, they did the same job as their parents. Girls didn't get to go to school; they were taught all they needed to know from their mothers and helped with any work at home.

26

TOYS

When they weren't busy working and learning, children played with lots of different toys. Toys were usually made of clay and were shaped like animals. Some girls were given special paddle dolls. These dolls were thought to be magical and helped to make sure that girls had children when they grew up.

Paddle doll

Hippo toy

Some people were buried with paddle dolls.

WEDDING BELLS

Girls got married when they were around 12 years old and boys got married when they were a bit older. There weren't big weddings. Instead, people were considered married when a woman walked into her new husband's house. Husbands and wives could split up if they wanted to.

27

Crime and Punishment

Laws were pretty simple in ancient Egypt – if you did the crime, then you might pay with your life. Other punishments included beatings, stabbings or being burnt alive. However, even with these punishments, people still committed crimes.

NO NOSE, NO EARS, NO PROBLEMS

Crimes such as stealing could be met with your body being mutilated. This means having a body part cut off. It was often your ears or your nose.

It's fine – we can just glue it back on, right? RIGHT?

Hands up who caught a criminal today.

MONKEYING AROUND

The police sometimes had trained monkeys with them. They were trained to attack thieves who tried to **FLEE** the scene of the crime.

28

POWER TO THE SNITCH

If you thought the criminals had it bad, you should see how we treated people who saw crimes. If somebody saw a crime, they had to tell the police what they saw. People who didn't tell anyone when they saw a crime could be punished.

Where are those WITNESSES? I'm ready to whip!

BEAT THE WITNESS

We believed that people who had been ACCUSED of a crime were GUILTY until proven INNOCENT. To check whether a person was guilty or innocent, witnesses were beaten to make sure that they told the truth.

PERSONALISED PUNISHMENTS

Witnesses would be forced to swear to the gods they were telling the truth. They would also have to outline what would happen to them if they were found to be lying.

29

Senebti!

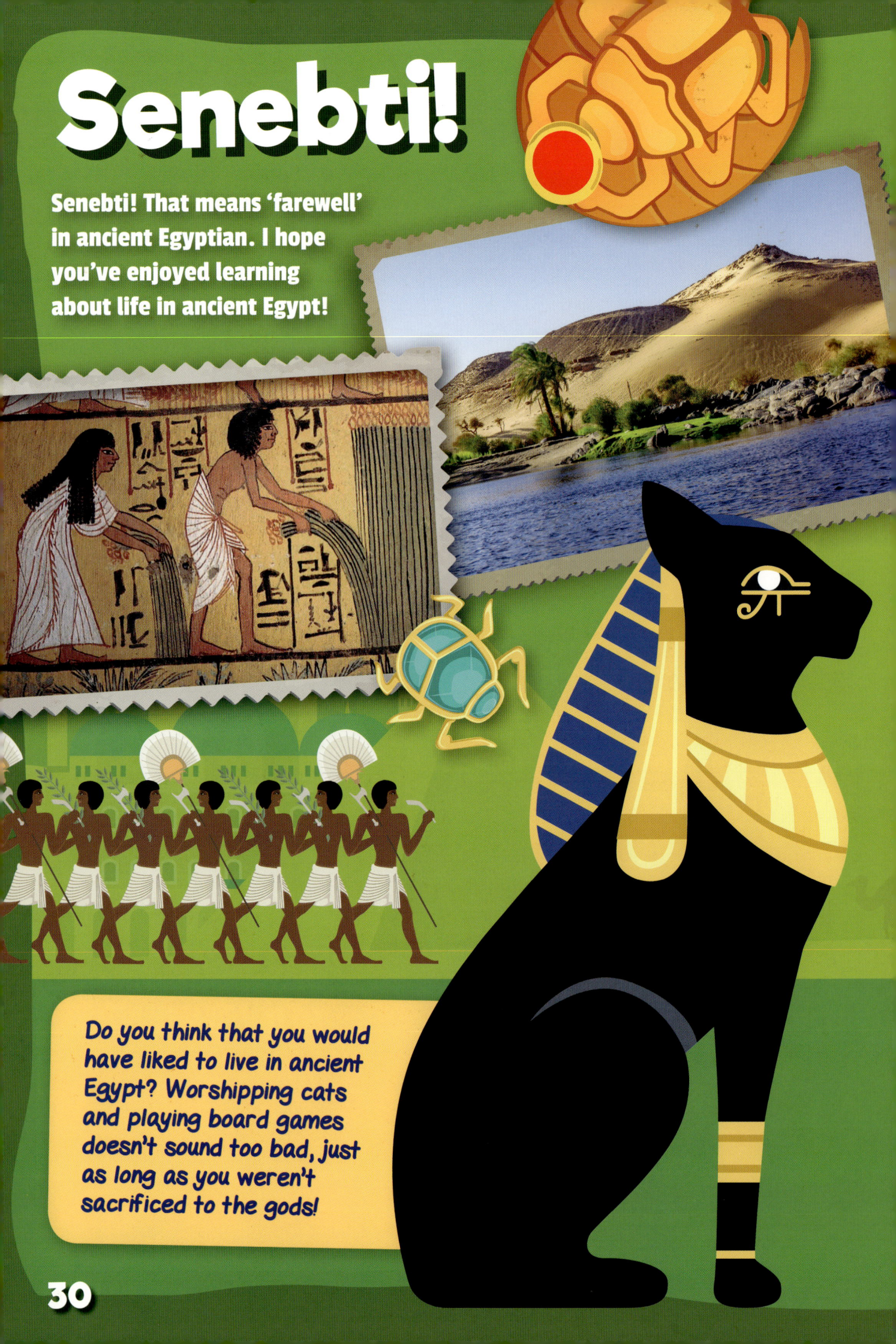

Senebti! That means 'farewell' in ancient Egyptian. I hope you've enjoyed learning about life in ancient Egypt!

Do you think that you would have liked to live in ancient Egypt? Worshipping cats and playing board games doesn't sound too bad, just as long as you weren't sacrificed to the gods!

ACCUSED charged with committing a crime or doing something wrong

ADOPT to make someone part of a family by choice instead of being related to the family

AFTERLIFE a religious belief that there is life after death

AMULETS pieces of jewellery thought to protect the wearer against evil, danger or disease

BC meaning 'before Christ', it is used to mark the dates that occurred before the starting year of most calendars

CHANNELS long, narrow trenches or tubes that things can flow through

CHAOS a state of disorder and confusion

CIVILISATION the society, culture and way of life of a certain area

DIARRHOEA runny poo

FERTILE able to support the growth and life of plants

FLEE run away from

GUILTY responsible for a certain bad action or wrongdoing

HARVESTED the process of gathering crops

HOOVES the hard part on the feet of some animals such as horses, pigs and deer

INNOCENT not responsible or guilty of something

JACKAL a type of dog that is closely related to wolves

LAXATIVES things that cause people to go to the toilet (for a poo) when eaten

LICE small creatures that can live on the bodies of larger animals including humans

LIMESTONE a type of hard, sedimentary rock

LINEN a type of fabric that is made from the flax plant

MINES deep holes made in the earth from which gold, coal or precious metals can be dug out

MOURN to feel grief or pain for someone that has died

MYRRH an expensive plant extract that is often used to make perfume

NATRON a type of salt that soaks up water

ORGANS parts of a living thing that have specific, important jobs to do

PRESERVED kept in its original form

RAZORS sharp blades that can be used to remove hair

RECORDS documents or files which keep track of something

RITUALS ordered actions that take place during religious ceremonies

SACRIFICED when animals or people are killed and offered to a god or gods

SCEPTRE a long staff or stick that represents someone's power

SERPENT a type of large snake

TAXES payments made to the government so that they can provide services

TEMPLES places of worship

WITNESSES people who were there at the time a crime happened

INDEX

A
afterlife 10–11, 17, 20

B
burial 11, 14, 17, 27

C
cats 18
children 6, 17, 22, 26–27
cities 5
coffins 11
crime 9, 28–29
crocodiles 8, 19

D
dogs 18–20

F
flies 15, 25

G
giraffes 25
gods 5–12, 14, 18, 20, 26, 29

H
hair 17
hieroglyphs 22–23
hippos 20, 27
houses 5, 24–25, 27

L
lice 17, 23
lions 6, 18–20

M
monkeys 19, 28
mummies 6, 8, 10–11

P
paper 23
papyrus 21, 23, 25
pets 18–19
pharaohs 4–5, 8, 11, 14–16
priests 5, 8, 11

R
River Nile 4, 9, 16, 23

S
sarcophagi 11, 23
school 22, 26
scribes 5, 22
senet 20
serpent 11, 20
sheep 6, 17
slaves 5, 15
Sun, the 6–7, 9
sunlight 16, 24

T
teeth 12–13, 16
toothpaste 16
toys 27

W
wigs 17
women 6, 17, 27
writing 5–6, 22–23